String Quartet

John Kember

Chanson de matin

8 Twentieth-Century Pieces Arranged for String Quartet

ED 12844
ISMN M-2201-2365-8

www.schott-music.com

Mainz · London · Madrid · New York · Paris · Prague · Tokyo · Toronto
© 2006 Schott & Co. Ltd, London · Printed in Germany

Contents

ED 12844
British Library Cataloguing-in-Publication Data.
A catalogue record for this book is available from the British Library
ISMN M-2201-2365-8

Cover design and typesetting by www.adamhaystudio.com
Music setting by Figaro
Printed in Germany S&Co.8027

1. Chanson de matin

Op. 15, No. 2

arr. John Kember

Edward Elgar
(1857–1934)

2. Pie Jesu

from *Requiem*

arr. John Kember

Gabriel Fauré
(1845–1924)

3. La Calinda

from *Koanga* (abridged)

arr. John Kember

Frederick Delius
(1862–1934)

4. Nimrod

arr. John Kember

Adagio

from the *Enigma Variations*, Op. 36

Edward Elgar
(1857–1934)

5. Brigg Fair

arr. John Kember

(Abridged)

Frederick Delius
(1862–1934)

With easy movement ♩. = 66

John Kember

Chanson de matin

8 Twentieth-Century Pieces Arranged for String Quartet

ED 12844
ISMN M-2201-2365-8

Mainz · London · Madrid · New York · Paris · Prague · Tokyo · Toronto
© 2006 Schott & Co. Ltd, London · Printed in Germany

ED 12844
British Library Cataloguing-in-Publication Data.
A catalogue record for this book is available from the British Library
ISMN M-2201-2365-8

Cover design and typesetting by www.adamhaystudio.com
Music setting by Figaro
Printed in Germany S&Co.8027

Contents

1. Chanson de Matin

Op. 15, No. 2

arr. John Kember

Edward Elgar
(1857–1934)

2. Pie Jesu

from *Requiem*

arr. John Kember

Gabriel Fauré
(1845–1924)

3. La Calinda

from *Koanga* (abridged)

arr. John Kember

Frederick Delius
(1862–1934)

4. Nimrod

from the *Enigma Variations*, Op. 36

arr. John Kember

Edward Elgar
(1857–1934)

5. Brigg Fair

(Abridged)

arr. John Kember

Frederick Delius
(1862–1934)

6. Folk Song Prelude No. 2

arr. John Kember

Peter Warlock
(1894–1930)

7. Morgenstemning

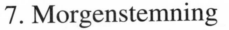

Morgenstimmung – Le matin – Morning mood

arr. John Kember

Edvard Grieg
(1843–1907)

8. The Angel's Farewell

from *The Dream of Gerontius*

arr. John Kember

Edward Elgar
(1857–1934)

John Kember

Chanson de matin

8 Twentieth-Century Pieces Arranged for String Quartet

ED 12844
ISMN M-2201-2365-8

www.schott-music.com

Mainz · London · Madrid · New York · Paris · Prague · Tokyo · Toronto
© 2006 Schott & Co. Ltd, London · Printed in Germany

ED 12844
British Library Cataloguing-in-Publication Data.
A catalogue record for this book is available from the British Library
ISMN M-2201-2365-8

© 2006 Schott & Co. Ltd, London

Cover design and typesetting by www.adamhaystudio.com
Music setting by Figaro
Printed in Germany S&Co.8027

Contents

1. Chanson de Matin

Op. 15, No. 2

arr. John Kember

Edward Elgar
(1857–1934)

2. Pie Jesu

from *Requiem*

arr. John Kember

Gabriel Fauré
(1845–1924)

3. La Calinda

from *Koanga* (abridged)

arr. John Kember

Frederick Delius
(1862–1934)

4. Nimrod

arr. John Kember

from the *Enigma Variations*, Op. 36

Edward Elgar
(1857–1934)

5. Brigg Fair

(Abridged)

arr. John Kember

Frederick Delius
(1862–1934)

6. Folk Song Prelude No. 2

arr. John Kember

Peter Warlock
(1894–1930)

7. Morgenstemning

Morgenstimmung – Le matin – Morning mood

arr. John Kember

Edvard Grieg
(1843–1907)

Allegretto pastorale ♩ = 60

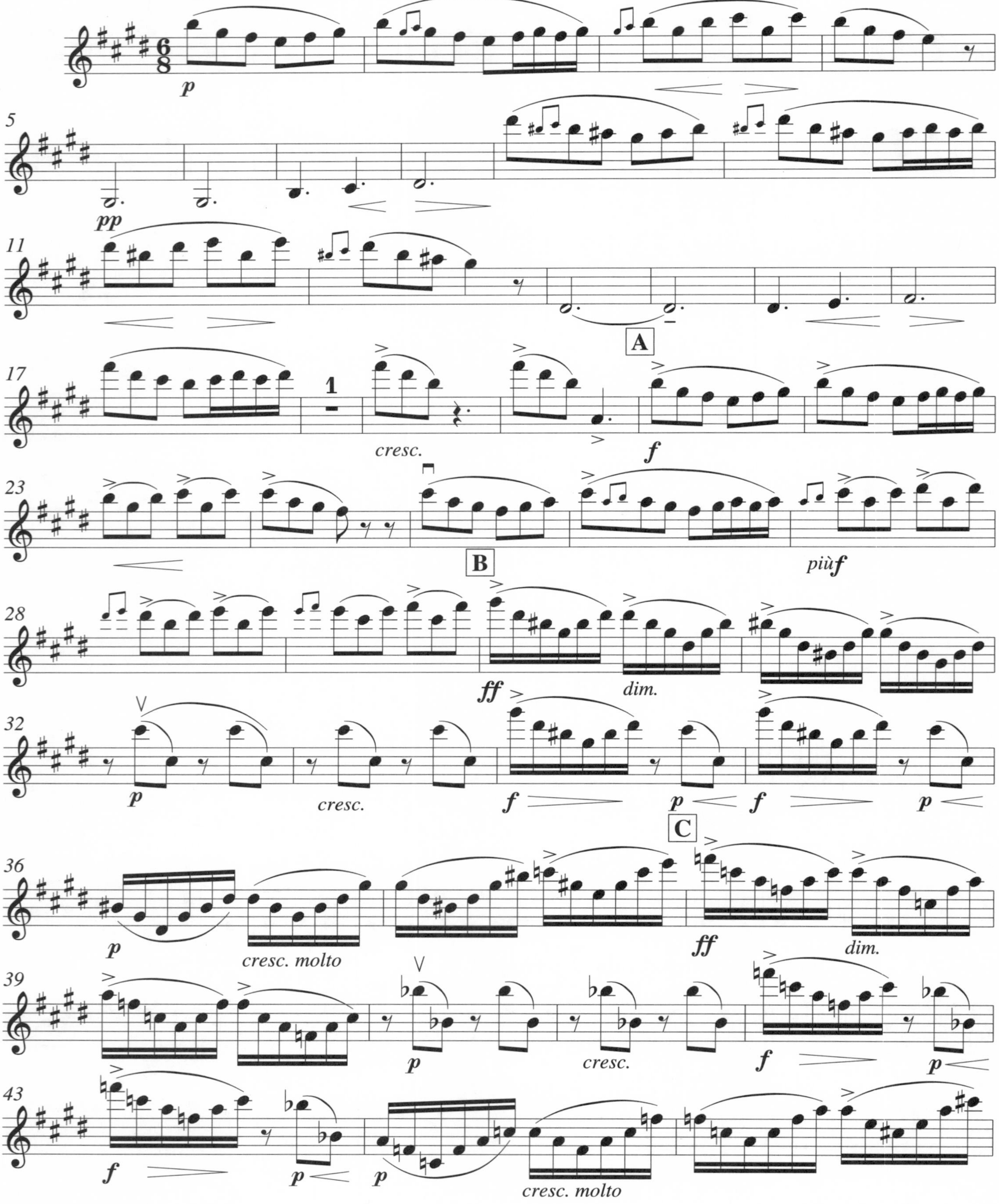

8. The Angel's Farewell

from *The Dream of Gerontius*

arr. John Kember

Edward Elgar
(1857–1934)

S&Co.8027 Printed in Germany

John Kember

Chanson de matin

8 Twentieth-Century Pieces Arranged for String Quartet

ED 12844
ISMN M-2201-2365-8

www.schott-music.com

Mainz · London · Madrid · New York · Paris · Prague · Tokyo · Toronto
© 2006 Schott & Co. Ltd, London · Printed in Germany

ED 12844
British Library Cataloguing-in-Publication Data.
A catalogue record for this book is available from the British Library
ISMN M-2201-2365-8

Cover design and typesetting by www.adamhaystudio.com
Music setting by Figaro
Printed in Germany S&Co.8027

Contents

1. Chanson de Matin

Op. 15, No. 2

arr. John Kember

Edward Elgar
(1857–1934)

2. Pie Jesu

arr. John Kember

from *Requiem*

Gabriel Fauré
(1845–1924)

Adagio ♩ = 44

3. La Calinda

from *Koanga* (abridged)

arr. John Kember

Frederick Delius
(1862–1934)

4. Nimrod

arr. John Kember

from the *Enigma Variations*, Op. 36

Edward Elgar
(1857–1934)

5. Brigg Fair

(Abridged)

arr. John Kember

Frederick Delius
(1862–1934)

6. Folk Song Prelude No. 2

arr. John Kember

Peter Warlock
(1894–1930)

Violin II

7. Morgenstemning

Morgenstimmung – Le matin – Morning mood

arr. John Kember

Edvard Grieg
(1843–1907)

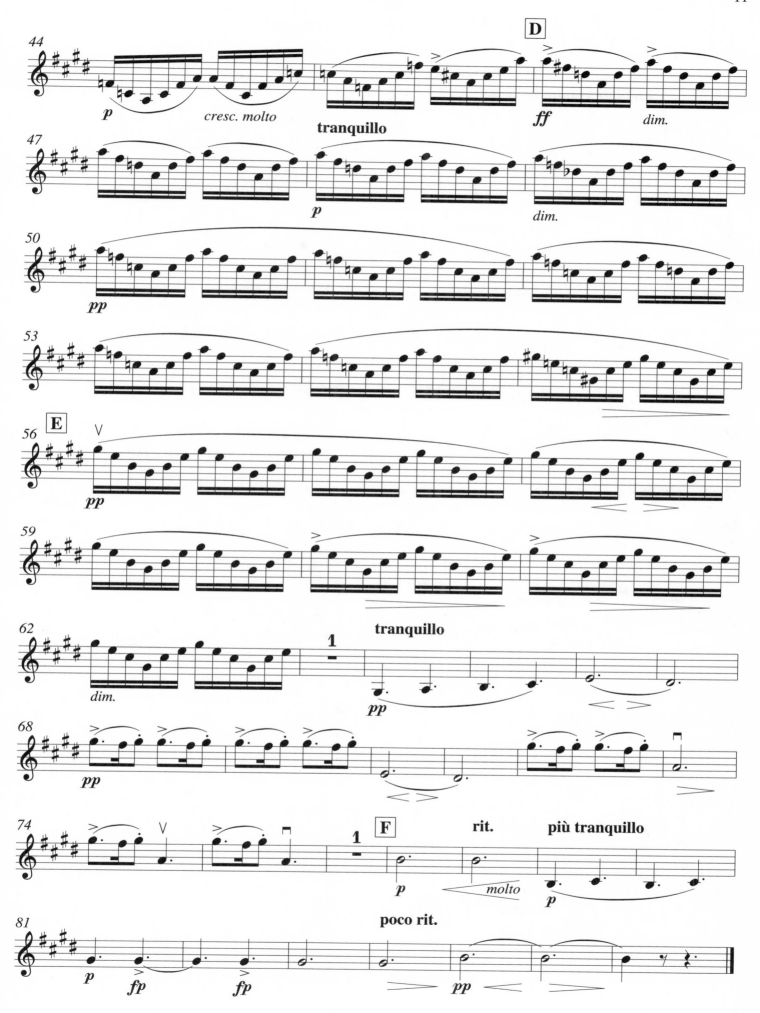

8. The Angel's Farewell

from *The Dream of Gerontius*

arr. John Kember

Edward Elgar
(1857–1934)

John Kember

Chanson de matin

8 Twentieth-Century Pieces Arranged for String Quartet

ED 12844
ISMN M-2201-2365-8

www.schott-music.com

Mainz · London · Madrid · New York · Paris · Prague · Tokyo · Toronto
© 2006 Schott & Co. Ltd, London · Printed in Germany

ED 12844
British Library Cataloguing-in-Publication Data.
A catalogue record for this book is available from the British Library
ISMN M-2201-2365-8

© 2006 Schott & Co. Ltd, London

Cover design and typesetting by www.adamhaystudio.com
Music setting by Figaro
Printed in Germany S&Co.8027

Contents

Violoncello

1. Chanson de Matin

Op. 15, No. 2

Edward Elgar
(1857–1934)

arr. John Kember

2. Pie Jesu

from *Requiem*

arr. John Kember

Gabriel Fauré
(1845–1924)

3. La Calinda

from *Koanga* (abridged)

arr. John Kember

Frederick Delius
(1862–1934)

75

pp

83

4. Nimrod

arr. John Kember

from the *Enigma Variations*, Op. 36

Edward Elgar
(1857–1934)

Adagio

pp

8

p   *cresc.*   *mf*

16

sonore   *dim.*   *p*

23

p   *cresc.*   *mf*   *f*

29

cresc.   *ff*

largando   **molto rit.**

36

sf   *ff*   *pp*

5. Brigg Fair

(Abridged)

arr. John Kember

Frederick Delius
(1862–1934)

Più vivo

rather slower and dying away

6. Folk Song Prelude No. 2

arr. John Kember

Peter Warlock
(1894–1930)

7. Morgenstemning

Morgenstimmung – Le matin – Morning mood

arr. John Kember

Edvard Grieg
(1843–1907)

8. The Angel's Farewell

from *The Dream of Gerontius*

arr. John Kember

Edward Elgar
(1857–1934)

S&Co.8027 Printed in Germany

rather slower and dying away

6. Folk Song Prelude No. 2

arr. John Kember

Peter Warlock
(1894–1930)

7. Morgenstemning

Morgenstimmung – Le matin – Morning mood

arr. John Kember

Edvard Grieg
(1843–1907)

8. The Angel's Farewell

arr. John Kember

from *The Dream of Gerontius*

Edward Elgar
(1857–1934)